GRAMPS
the AWESOME Otter

Written by Kathryn Lentz
Illustrated by Stephanie Richoll

MyFourHawks PUBLISHING

Copyright © 2020, Kathryn Lentz

All rights reserved. No part of this publication may be reproduced, distributed, or transmitted in any form or by any means, including photocopying, recording, or other electronic or mechanical methods, without the prior written permission of the publisher, except in the case of brief quotations embodied in critical reviews and certain other noncommercial uses permitted by copyright law. For permission requests, write to the publisher, addressed "Attention: Permissions Coordinator," at the address below.

MyFourHawks PUBLISHING

Kathryn Lentz
Chicago, Illinois
myfourhawks@gmail.com
kathrynlentz.com

Illustrator: Stephanie Richoll
Photographer: Kathryn Lentz
Editor: Shayla Raquel, shaylaraquel.com
Formatting: Martin Publishing Services, martinpublishingservices.com

ISBN:
978-1-7348151-0-8 (paperback)
978-1-7348151-1-5 (hardback)
978-7348151-2-2 (epub)

*To my grandchildren:
you are my endless joy.
I see the best of our families
in each of you.*

Otters live in Alaska—a frozen playground—
swimming near Sitka, Wrangell,
and in Prince William Sound.
I paddle from town most every nice day
to a place I love called Frosty Bay.

Shorey Teller
NeighNeigh
BLUE BUTTERFLY
Pick Six
Frosty Bay, Ak

I visit otters to study their ways,
like floating in seaweed that looks like a maze.

Gramps is my favorite and lives near the bay.
He greets every boat as they sail away.

People who fish look to Gramps for good luck.
So their catch of the day will fill a big truck.

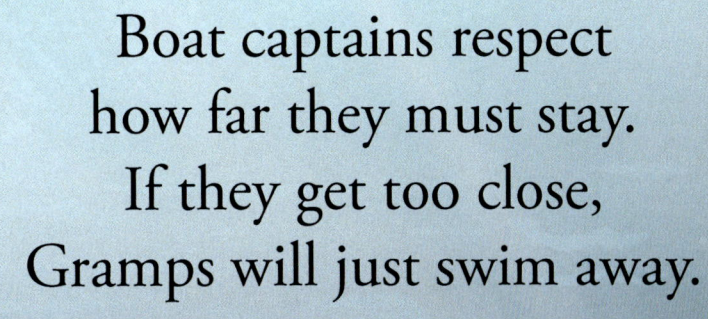

Boat captains respect
how far they must stay.
If they get too close,
Gramps will just swim away.

Perfect Together

Children on tours give each other high fives
when they watch Gramps as he flips and dives.
He gives them great memories of life in the wild
that someday they'll tell to their own little child.

Everyone here knows
Gramps is the one
to care for his friends
and have so much fun.

Gramps swims in the surf
at five miles an hour
against those big waves.
It takes so much power!

He joins other otters
in groups we call rafts.
They hold hands to rest—
now how cute is that?

Otters gather in seaweed
that we call kelp.
It keeps rafts together—
what a big help!

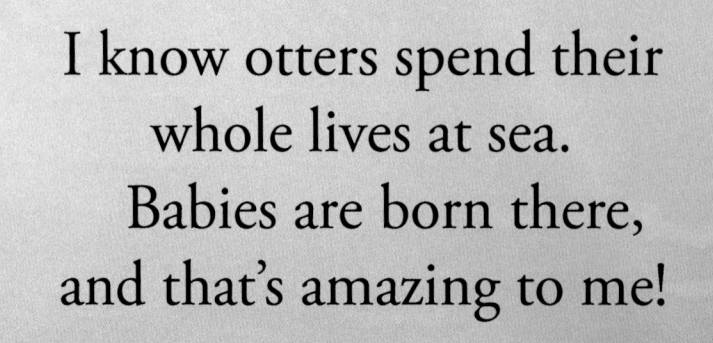

I know otters spend their
whole lives at sea.
Babies are born there,
and that's amazing to me!

Gramps and his pals
can dive 300 feet,
moving boulders and shells
and finding starfish to greet.

Each square inch of fur has one million hairs.
That's more than your dog or reindeer or bears!

Otters are social and chatter all day.
They whistle and squeal and have lots to say.

Gramps carries a tool he puts under his arm.
A rock to break shells, it works like a charm.

I know Gramps well—he's the star of the sea.
I'm happy to see him living wild and free.

Otterly Awesome Otter Facts

1. A sea otter that weighs 80 pounds has to eat 20 pounds of food every day. If you weigh 80 pounds, you would have to eat 14 six-inch sub sandwiches each day to eat like an otter. If your parent weighs 140 pounds, he or she would have to eat 34 pounds of food each day. That's 74 sub sandwiches every day just to eat like an otter!

2. A baby otter lives on its mom's tummy for at least six months and can weigh 30 pounds.

3. Newborn otter fur is filled with so much air that they cannot go underwater, just like a balloon can't.

4. Moms wrap their babies in kelp to protect them when they leave to look for food.

5. When it's cloudy underwater and otters can't see, they feel vibrations with their whiskers to know a boulder or boat is nearby.

6. They must keep their fur clean to stay warm, so they spend a lot of time every day cleaning their fur with their tongues, like a cat.

7. Male otters can be four and a half feet long and weigh up to 100 pounds.

8. When otters get older, their faces turn white. They are called "The Old Man of the Sea."

9. We have about 100,000 hairs on our heads. Otters have 1 million hairs every square inch. That's as much as an adult German shepherd has on its whole body.

10. Even though there are 70,000 sea otters in Alaskan waters, there used to be hundreds of thousands. That's why they are endangered.

Gramps loves where he lives.
How about you?

What fun is diving...

...without a big splash!

Resting after a day of ocean adventures.

Time for a nap.

Peek-A-Boo...I fooled you.

Gramps has taught us so much about how otters live.
I think Gramps is awesome and I think you're awesome too!

Acknowledgments

A big thank-you to all of you, in no particular order, whose patience I have tested from the inception to the printing of *Gramps the Awesome Otter*.

My professional team:

Shayla Raquel, my editor, for your guidance and direction.

Stephanie Richoll, my illustrator, for your artistic insight and creativity.

Melinda Martin, of Martin Publishing Services,
for your personal approach and skillful formatting.

I am grateful to be surrounded by your talent and knowledge.

Team Gramps:

Barbara Preiner, my friend and writing contributor.

Julius, my husband, my North Star.

Kristin and Carrie, my little girls. Now inspiring women.

Margaret DiVincenzo, my wonderfully wise best friend.

I truly appreciate all your advice and support.
I am blessed to have you in my life. I will simply say, "Thank you."

Alaska Wildlife Guides

In my humble opinion, the best of the best wildlife guides:

A Whale's Song Expeditions in Sitka, Alaska

Owner/Captain: Neil McDermott

Naturalist/Photographer: Lione Clare

Alaska Charters & Adventures in Wrangell, Alaska

Owners/Captains: John Yeager and Brenda Schwartz Yeager

Manager: Nancy Delpero

Captain/Guide: Michael Ottesen

Silver Salmon Creek Lodge in Lake Clark, Alaska

Owner/Captain: David Coray

Owner: Joanne Coray

The Unforgettable: Chewie

About the Author

Kathryn Lentz is a children's author, wildlife photographer, and animal educator. A retired pet groomer of thirty-seven years, she rescued dozens of dogs and cats to ensure every pet found wonderful homes with her clients. Through fifteen years of traveling in the US, Kathy has dedicated her time to learning more about animals and nature, which inspired her debut children's book, *Gramps the Awesome Otter*. When she's not snapping photos of adorable animals, you can find her spoiling her four grandkids, painting with oils, or teaching classrooms about their own wildlife environments. Kathy lives in a suburb of Chicago with her amazing husband, two dogs, and a cat. Connect with her at kathrynlentz.com.

About the Illustrator

Stephanie Richoll is a Florida native jack-of-all-trades artist. Graduating from Florida State University with a degree in Studio Art, Stephanie is now an established illustrator, painter, and graphic designer.

She has worked with several publishers and producers and has illustrated several published children's books and novels.

She hopes to travel the world, but for now is working with clients all over the world and hopes to continue producing art for amazing projects in the future.

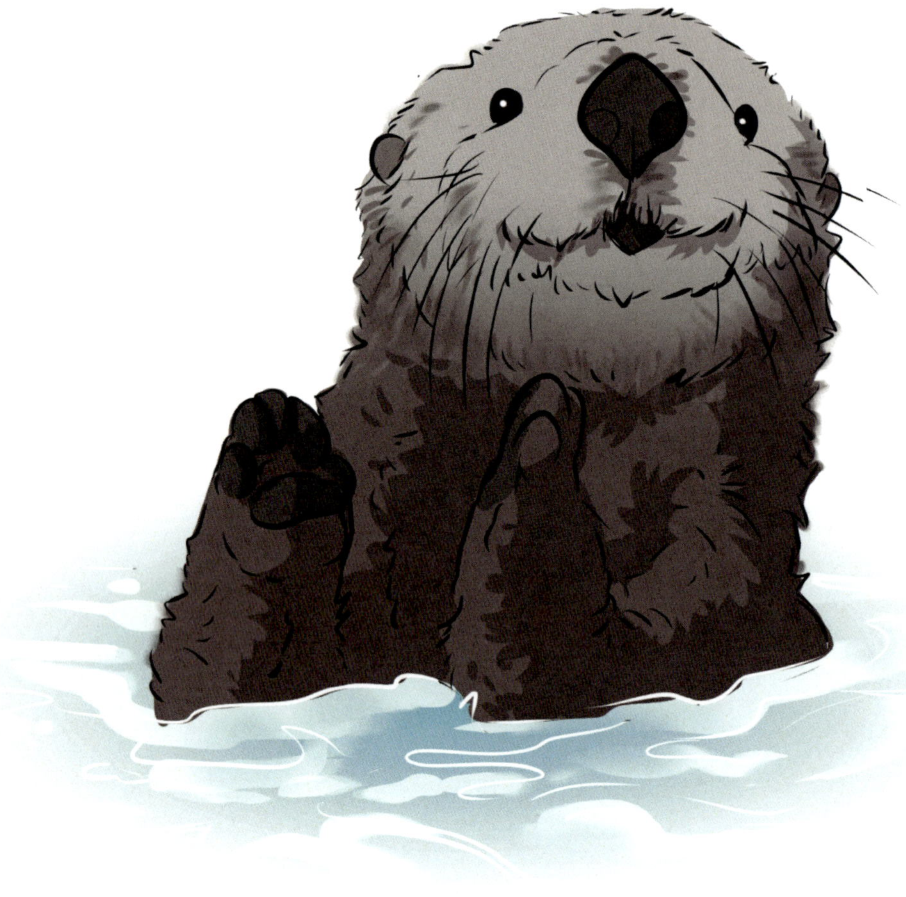

Manufactured by Amazon.ca
Bolton, ON